VISION ON PLATFORM 2

VISION ON PLATFORM 2

NANCY MATTSON

All rights reserved. No part of this work covered by the copyright herein may be reproduced or used in any means—graphic, electronic, or mechanical, including copying, recording, taping, or information storage and retrieval systems—without written permission of the publisher.

Printed by imprintdigital
Upton Pyne, Exeter
www.digital.imprint.co.uk

Typesetting and cover design by narrator
www.narrator.me.uk
info@narrator.me.uk
033 022 300 39

Published by Shoestring Press
19 Devonshire Avenue, Beeston, Nottingham, NG9 1BS
(0115) 925 1827
www.shoestringpress.co.uk

First published 2018
© Copyright: Nancy Mattson
© Cover image, "Metro ligne N°8" [2008] oil on canvas, by Shelagh Hickman, Paris.

The moral right of the author has been asserted.

ISBN 978-1-912524-13-6

ACKNOWLEDGEMENTS

My thanks to the editors of the following publications in which some of these poems have appeared, sometimes in earlier versions: *Acumen*, *ARTEMISpoetry*, *Frogmore Papers*, *Interpreter's House*, *Journal of Franciscan Colleges and Universities*, *Other Poetry*, *Seam*; online poetry magazines *London Grip*, *Morphrog*, and *TRUCK*; anthologies *Days Begin … poetry in support of the Cancer Centre Campaign for Colchester* (Wivenbooks, 2015), *A Festschrift for Barry Cole* (Shoestring Press, 2015), *Herrings* (Blue Door Press and Poetry in Aldeburgh, 2017), *KG Confidential: A Festschrift for Katherine Gallagher* (Circle Time Press, 2015), *My Mother Threw Knives: Poems About Women's Lives* (Second Light Publications, 2006), *Poetry and All That Jazz* (Chichester Poetry Festival anthology, 2018), *so too have the doves gone: reflections on the theme of conflict* (Jardine Press, 2014), *Strike Up the Band: Poems for John Lucas at 80* (Plas Gwyn Books, 2017), *Towards the Light: Poems of reconciliation* (Kapaju Books, 2018).

"Little Mother" and "Other Mothers" won first and second prize in the 2013 St Edmundsbury Cathedral Poetry Competition.

The following poems were commended: "At the Elbow of Pissarro" (2008 Bedford Open Poetry Competition), "Betrayal of the Larynx" (2016 Torbay Poetry Competition), "Goatfell, Isle of Arran" (2010 Ware Poetry Competition), "Her Habit" and "Voyages" (Torriano Poetry Competition 2013 and 2012).

I am deeply grateful to Rebecca Goss and Michael Bartholomew-Biggs for their thoughtful criticism and invaluable help in shaping this collection. My thanks also to John Lucas and others who have commented incisively on individual poems, including Graham Claydon, Margaret Hollingsworth, Fawzia Kane, Paul Richards, Anna Robinson, John Roe, Katherine Venn and the late Carol Hughes.

My heartfelt thanks to my husband, Michael Bartholomew-Biggs, whose endless love, support, encouragement, patience, and literary sensitivity never cease to surprise me.

Many thanks to Shelagh Hickman for her kind permission to reproduce "Metro ligne N°8" on the front cover of this collection.

CONTENTS

I

Wading for stones	3
Stuff in a memory, pull out a thread	4
Braids	6
See the pyramids along the Nile	7
Little mother	8
Voyages	9
Our house is called 5212	10
The man in the basement suite at 5212	12
Reveen the Impossibilist	14
In praise of lazy rivers	15
Widow, marooned	16
Canadian apple elegy, or looking back to Adanac	17
Nothing to see here	18

II

The brothers' vow, 1946	21
Betrayal of the larynx	22
'Karhu' means bear but you must not say it here	23
What the carver heard	24
Her decision	26
Epitaph, floating	27
Threads for a woman priest	28
Overture	29
My grandmother did not speak of moths	30
Drinking at the Stray Dog Cabaret	32
Idaho women	33
Pen and ink	34
Miracle on Essex Road	35
Other mothers	36
Expecting no welcome	38
Into the west with Ravilious and you	39
Winter anniversary in Bruges	41

Anonymous 'Flemish Primitive'
(almost certainly male) depicts Pentecost 42
You asked God for a dream 44
Goatfell, Isle of Arran 45
Her family 46

III

Shadow in Hadleigh 49
At the elbow of Pissarro 50
Vision on Platform 2 52
Her habit 54
In search of uplift 56
How to translate joy 57
Every seventh starling 58
Goldfinch 59
Fifteenth swan 60
Honeymoon flight, circa 1934 61
Sunday morning in Bergamo with Damon 62
A soldier ponders the limits of arithmetic 64
Stones on trial 65
The cape and the steeple 66
Feast 67

Notes 68
Author Biography 69

For Mike, with love

I

*In the pause between the first draft and the carbon
they glimpse the smooth hours when they were children—*
— P. K. Page

WADING FOR STONES

I must have thrown away
chip by chip
a whole sequoia
twelve million years old
when I was a kid.

I must have scooped up
a jawful of teeth
lost one by one by
prehistoric horses
when I was a kid.

I saved them until
they struck me as ugly
on my windowsill
the year I took up
jiving and lipstick.

Who would cast off
treasures the river gives?

Now I wade in the shallows
of the gravelly Saskatchewan
hoping for even one chunk
of petrified wood,
one stone tooth.

Barefoot on a wide sandbar,
ankled in silt, flour gold,
mastodon bones puréed
by glaciers, I'm building
mudtowns with grandchildren

who capture minnows, float
canoe-leaves on the river
the Blackfoot people say
Wesakechak made
when God was a kid.

STUFF IN A MEMORY, PULL OUT A THREAD

After Louise Bourgeois

Memories come unstitched.
Here's a leather pommel horse,
rancid from sweat and teachers' scorn.

With the pointed fury of a girl wronged,
I aim my body at the horse again, touch
the springboard with clever toes: one bounce

and steel arms carry my torso straight up
like a spiral bobbin, twisting, re-winding
until I straddle the horse, splay my legs, pause

above it like a hovering wishbone. Hold time still.
Only then can I raise my knees, click my heels
tight for the dismount, hit the mat crisp.

A thousand hours to learn the art of jumping true,
how to land upright after two hard heel-thunks,
arms in a high V. Time to cut the cord on that lie.

*

Caught between the crotch of scissors
in this gallery and blood that gushes
under the studio door

I am pulled by an uncut cord into the pinhole
between my mother's legs, my own,
my daughter's legs, my own.

Thanks to smooth screws at the X-joints
two sets of scissor-legs and finger-holes
open and shut, kissety-clack, repeat.

Although my mother taught me
the art of separation—spread,
squeeze and cut—bits of thread still dangle.

I showed my daughter what to do—
open, shut and snip—but she ran away
with the scissors, ripping the cord.

*

No more sucking and swallowing dust-balls.
Pupuus' my mother called them, only lips and breath.
She had a soft way of saying p's like b's.

When I pull the plug-head out of its wall-socket,
press a button to release something mechanical
inside the vacuum-belly—ratchet or pulley

or spring-lock—the cord whips along the floor,
snaps into its secret hoover-hole.
Let no one call me a dirty woman.

BRAIDS

Braids have purposes, they know
from the scalp, their source
that they will end

in flimsiness, a tail swish
as hair gives way
                to air

I remember my mother
braiding my hair, the ritual
of scoring my scalp with a steel
                        rat-tail

I did not squirm
        My skull hurt
                Each hair, root to tip
                had to learn its place

This tarnished mirror remembers bright
fat plaits that narrowed
dwindled
faded

                like feather tips
                or wisps of whale baleen
                for sifting krill

                like the skirt of a worn-out
                dancer, her ragged hems sodden
                as she waded into the sea

SEE THE PYRAMIDS ALONG THE NILE

A small black case
lined in orange velvet

packets of strings in permanent curls
plectrums as soft as babies' nails

a chrome yellow Bakelite box
three fingers wide

her Pyramid Pitch Pipe
for violin and mandolin

my mother's lip prints
on these whistle pipes

each as long as my thumb
each with an old reed

I need to wet
with new spit

her fingerprints
on this mandolin

a red ribbon round
its neck to hang it

I no longer squirm
to call this ribbon scarlet

and welcome all those songs
that stuck in my craw before

her arm and leg went stone
her voice went monotone

LITTLE MOTHER

Miriam gathered strips of papyrus
trimmed from pages glued by scribes

cut her thumb-size dolls in folded
rows of sisters holding hands

Miriam painted their shifts with crumbs
of cast-off pigments wetted with spit

arranged her paper passengers
in egg-size boats she wove from reeds

like the belly-size boat her mother made
lined with linen and sealed with pitch

Miriam floated her dolls in the Nile
beside her infant brother, *Goodbye!*

She raced the current as far as the bridge
leaving her mother crumpled on the bank

VOYAGES

Girls and boys, go out to play
but don't go near the slough.
At the edges of cities
behind nettle fences
we salvaged planks and two-by-fours
dumped in the reeds by ne'er-do-wells,
prised out rusty nails with crowbars,
tied the boards to cast-off tires
with binder twine and scout-knots.

Don't swim in the reservoir,
remember your cousin who drowned?
Eight years older and ten years gone,
he couldn't stop us from launching coracles
on foetid water, telling our own stories
of equator-crossing captains, conquerors
who took booty back to Spain or England:
gold and tobacco, dancing aboriginals
with painted bodies, feathered crowns.

Don't be late for supper
or it's only bread and water.
Sailing through centuries
until our rafts were swamped,
we waded through mud and weeds,
broken bottles and crocodiles,
holding our innocent gumboots
high above our heads.

OUR HOUSE IS CALLED 5212

In my favourite books, houses and streets have names
but here it's all numbers. Our house is called 5212.
I wish it could be Cherryvale Cottage, but no
I'd have to name it Chokecherry House.

Brown Stucco Duplex would sound silly.
We live on 106 Street (my dad says *hunnert-an-six*)
but I want Pine Lane or Poplar Street. Or what about
Caragana Avenue? Sounds nice, and it's true.

Last year we lived in the red brick Ravina Apartments
on Villa Avenue, basement suite, phone 82207.
Once I went with Mom to the top floor to have tea
with the lady who had black numbers on her arm.

I'd play all day with my friends in the ravine,
pick saskatoons and raspberries to survive.
Chokecherries taste horrid (my mom says *kauhea*)
but you have to eat some, that's the rule. Your mouth

turns purple, your lips wrinkle, your tongue and throat
dry up, like chewing sand and burrs at the same time.
You can spit poison chokecherry pits at the other tribe,
squeal like little savages with purply-blue lips.

I know there's a 'p' in raspberry but it's silent.
I'm good at spelling and reading. Last autumn
on the neighbour's verandah the older boys
had a book with photos of people's bodies

piled up or stacked in rows on the ground
or in wagons. I didn't tell Mom what I saw.
This year we moved to the city limits,
I don't know why. Everything is flat here except

Mount Pleasant, you can see it from our kitchen.
It's the only cemetery I know. I walk by myself
up and down the hills, follow rows of trees.
My favourite is mountain ash, rare among the spruce.

Shadows of needles
scratch the gravestones,
leaves and berries
make wavy silhouettes.

My elementary fingers trace letters,
birth and death numbers,
sharp cuts into smooth slabs
of grey or black or rust-coloured stone.

My tongue sounds out men with names,
their wives, children, babies:
I can subtract in my head.

THE MAN IN THE BASEMENT SUITE AT 5212

hid magazines behind the octopus furnace.
Corinne and I found them by climbing over
the coal bin. We did everything together.

The covers of *Argosy, Stag, Real Men*
were sticky with black fingerprints
that smudged our hands and skirts.

We squinted at pistols, machetes,
rifles ending in blades. Tanks with crosses
of upside-down and backward Ls.

Jungle cats whose teeth could rip your hand off.
Men with eagles, snakes or daggers
on their muscles. Women with scarlet lips,

torn blouses, tangled hair, wrists tied up
to trees. Worse than anything
in Nancy Drew. We snuck out fairly fast.

He kept a German shepherd named Jimmy
locked in a kennel in a strip of scrubland
between 5212 and the old mink pens,

thick sharp nettles climbing up their stilts.
Once when Mom was having coffee with Betty
next door, Corinne and I stole pork chops

from the fridge to stop Jimmy's barking.
Spies and detectives are always on the lookout
for peculiar stuff, like that mound beyond

the last mink pen. We pulled back the tarp—
holy Moses—a blue speedboat named *Lorelei*,
with silver stripes, a 60-horse Mercury outboard.

The Mounties came next day, took him away
in handcuffs, a cigarette burning in his teeth.
His wife went crying after the police car

all the way down the caragana-lined driveway
at 5212—106 Street. She howled and her bare knees
hit the gravel hard. He never did look back.

REVEEN THE IMPOSSIBILIST

Every poster seduced us: his black lightning eyes,
a pair of galaxies twirling from his red silk shoulders.

We queued and stamped outside the Paramount,
our gloves knitted with ice, eyelashes heavy with frost mascara.

Prone to hypnosis? Not me, I scorned the hocus-pocus
of Reveen: impossible for him to fool my teenaged mind

sharpened by acid and flame in the chemistry lab.
My clever brain's a double helix, my ultimate plan

to carry the dropped banner of Crick and
Watson's forgotten sister, Rosalind Franklin.

*

Reveen dangled the moon from a golden chain,
his beard an obsidian blade, his whisper a spell

that beckoned twenty and me from velvet seats, we
floated onstage, roosted on chrome chairs, armless.

My boyfriend swore later I danced as a sugar plum fairy,
kicked off my snowboots and twirled *petipa, petipa*,

played an air violin, swung my elephant trunk
in a lumpen walk to the watering hole.

With a tongue-click Reveen froze us, so the story
goes, into a herd of horses caught mid-stride,

then clapped twice to melt us. I believed the story
at the time but had no memory of foolishness. Still don't.

When we drove to the ski hill, headlights off, heater on,
I swear the moon sprayed stars onto snow.

IN PRAISE OF LAZY RIVERS

Shallow and frivolous, braided rivers
    spread and splay, beguiling me
        flaunting uncountable channels

like floozies or boozers, long hair in tangles
    silk robes floating open to negligées
        gathering buttered crumbs on thighs

Give me slow rivers like the Rakaia anytime
    their only job to shine and reflect patches of blues
        embroider clouds in silver-threaded doubles

They pay no mind to power, refuse to hurry
    or squeeze through narrow chutes
        hello Waimakariri, thanks for moseying along

Lazy rivers have the leisure given them
    by wide plains, the space to deposit their silt
        like swept lines of sawdust in a gymnasium

where dozens of dancers sway
    in calisthenic unison, ribbons floating
        from boneless wrists

Braided rivers say we have no need
    to choose between water and ground
        we can simply meander

let the earth show through now and then
    ridges of stones as clavicles
        skeletons of long-ago streams

WIDOW, MAROONED

I woke this morning stretching, drew back the sun-bleached
curtains that had covered up the sky, rubbed my eyes:
there was no prairie where the prairie used to stretch
beyond the fences that enclosed our herds of cattle
when we branded them, releasing them to graze
unplanted grasses all the hot dry summer long.

Where has the prairie gone?

Our dependable creek is drowned in a lake, no
it's a sea that came from nowhere overnight:
never in any memory of mine
or any prairie tales our elders told
has water ever spread around this house
marooning anyone. The power's out

but the radio tells me all the rivers
from the Rockies to my heart, I mean
the heart of this continent, have overrun
my eyes, I mean their banks, and flooded plains
that floods have never covered until now.

Some unknown fury's sucking up the oceans
turning cheek against prevailing westerlies
and filling up the devil's cunning funnels
as he laughs and pours out
forty days and nights of rain
in a single day and night.

Why is that helicopter circling my roof?

Oh give me back the drought I want
a multitude of desiccating angels
to swoop down from the mountains
on a herd of shiny hoovers
to suck the prairies empty I am thirsty
for the dustbowl of my youth.

CANADIAN APPLE ELEGY, OR LOOKING BACK TO ADANAC

Antique apples are now called heirlooms
since hardly anyone grows them anymore
except in heritage apple orchards,
open air museums of hard fruit.

Wrapped in tissue, Canadian apples
used to be shipped around the world
in wooden crates adorned with painted
Rockies, grizzlies, Mounties, moose.

Lost to our 21st century tongues,
the old apples keep their savour
only in the crunch of nomenclature.
Is it too late to call them back? Let's try.

Adanac, Cabashea, Fallawater, Grimes   *(Fallawater, Grimes)*
Pomme Grise, Quinte, Northern Spy   *(Northern Spy)*
Seek-no-Further, Maiden Blush   *(Maiden Blush)*
Wolf River, Princess Louise, *come back*   *(All is forgiven now)*

NOTHING TO SEE HERE

but sadness of candlesticks   time-hardened runnelwax
tarnish of silverware   clockfaces glass-broken
blemish of twisted brass   cracking of china bowls

ripping of silkenware   covering chesterfields
thread-gutted carpetwool   not-quite-covering floorboards
staircases barred against   upclimb or downfall

ghosts of my ancestors   floating in dust-shrouded air
their heads behind glass   their eyes black-marbled
skin-hands tight-gloved   ring-fingers leather-hid

nothing to see here   no strangling of neck-collars
nothing to see here   no hatpins piercing velvet felt
nothing to see here   no heirlooms to claim

II

But the dark pines of your mind dip deeper
And you are sinking, sinking, sleeper
In an elementary world;
There is something down there and you want it told.
— Gwendolyn MacEwen

THE BROTHERS' VOW, 1946

We will tell our stories in wood,
take turns splitting and stacking
lengths of poplar and birch. Each log,
stick and twig is a story we must tell.

We will tell our stories in fire,
open the iron door of the sauna stove,
rake the ashes, wring papers under kindling,
throw in a couple of lucifers, watch the flames spread.

We will loosen our throats, prime our tongues
with rye whisky, the kind we couldn't get on leave
in Europe. Only ale, wine, grappa, gin. Six long years.
Cards, booze, anything to never quite forget.

We will tell our stories in water
on hot stones, let steam release the memories
we can bear to reveal only to each other. Truth skinned.
What we had to witness, what our weapons did,

   how we survived, full of guilt and hard
   need, empty of boasting.   Any tears
   will join this steam and this we swear:
   no one else will ever hear our words.

Mother of all steam,
heal us, take away the stench.
When the bottle is empty, the fire dead,
may the stars cool our skins, the fireflies

   rekindle some of what we've lost
   as we hold each other up
   on the path toward the lamp
   in our mother's kitchen window.

BETRAYAL OF THE LARYNX

When I tried to speak on the phone
out of my throat came crows
in battle for the harbour.

When I tried to form words
out came the clank of masts,
the scratch of hooks,
hawser through a cat hole.

I used to work in lumber camps:
when a logger's blade loses its edge
it whines, inch by shredded inch
through the base of a tree.
I choked on splinters,
swallowed sawdust.

I know the ache of a pine
that surrenders branch
by branch. I remember
spine, neck and trunk
buckling into silence
on the forest floor.

Woodman spare me.

Give me a pen:
my tongue, my voice
and all my songs are gone,
my larynx split like cedar kindling.

'KARHU' MEANS BEAR BUT YOU MUST NOT SAY IT HERE

i. Eino the farmer to Veikko the client:

The sound of human talk warns off old Honey-Paw.
We stay silent in his forest, whisper in the hide.
Its tall chimney pipe carries away the scent of human breath.
Every day my boy and I go net fishing, haul in lake salmon
to entice Forest-Apple. My boy drives the tractor at dawn,
his trailer loaded with raw pink and silver to drop
at the foot of trees. Crows and gulls grab their fill
before handsome Honey-Paw comes sniffing.
But summer's over, the Wise Fellows are almost
full enough to burp. It's your last day to watch them
through binoculars, catch them on your digital SLR.
Tomorrow the hunting season opens.

ii. Veikko to his boy:

I'm no expert but I'll teach you to pad through the forest
on little cat-feet. We'll have to be clever to stalk old Otso,
canniest of all Karelian Kings. If he senses us and turns,
we'll hold our breath, keep our hoods down:
the Forest King can spot a glint of human eye-white
behind a peep-sight, hear that moment of excitement
before the hair-trigger click. Wise old Otso knows
the hunter's ways. He's bound to give your ego the slip,
mock your eagerness. Maybe you'll spot a yearling
without a name or reputation, too young for fear.
But even if you have a clear shot, hold your fire.
You can't take Mielikki's Sooty Boy.
Better to come home empty-handed
than have the wardens catch you.
You'd have to hide your first kill,
leave him face down on the forest floor.
That would dishonour you both, my son.

WHAT THE CARVER HEARD

After 'Two Totems' by Robert Koenig, Gibberd Garden

1

I'm a runner who carries messages
to overlords and lovers:
you may read these notes
to a future carved in wood

I'm a dancer complete
in the joy of my limbs:
you may hear my wooden toes
tap to the music of the wind

I'm a warrior who throws
spears and stones at my foes:
you may see their burial mounds
covered with lichens and moss

I'm a fisherman who shadows
the shoreline so lightly that fish
swim to find me, leap into my hands:
you can smell them cooking in the campfire

2

I had a woman once when we were young
who shaped me into a ridged log
thick as the base of a tree
two centuries old

I found a little nub
hidden in her undergrowth
and together, sap to leaf to sapling
we made this forest spread

3

Male and female maple we were made:
when the fluid in our roots and limbs
is ripe for tapping, you may pierce our skins
hang buckets on our torsos

Liquid will drip from our veins
for you to boil and clarify, throw on snow:
you may read your future in accidental patterns
your children may taste our syrup on their tongues

HER DECISION

They will come again, she fears.
The torso of this totem pole
is thicker than the hard belly
of this pregnant girl who kneels
at its foot, tracing crosses

around its girth, slicing her forefinger
in the incisions—carved smiles,
grimaces—that the sculptor chiselled
with blades sharp as the broken bottle
they threatened to use on her face.

They will come again, she fears.
She hears water, follows its sound
ripening through a shaded passage.
A waterfall beckons, a deep pool waits.

She drops in the copper ring
scored with a cross that the leader
gave her to seal his false troth.
He will never hear his child wail.

EPITAPH, FLOATING

> *When the epoch is buried*
> *no psalm is sung over the grave.*
> *Nettles and thistles will decorate it.*
> – Anna Akhmatova

Believe if you can that she fell near a stream
Know if you must she is buried in a wood
Hope that a friend marked the spot with a stone
    and that her name is carved upon it
Bury your fear she was lost in a field
Trust foxes and deer to visit her grave
Assume that nettles and thistles adorn it
    and that snow and wind sing antiphons

THREADS FOR A WOMAN PRIEST

The Word became thread
and wrapped around us,
woven loose for breathing,
strong in grace and truth.

So tell me something colourful,
pray me something bold,
murmur something liminal,
whisper something old.

Tell me something feminist,
rational, wild, how to
honour the sacred,
cherish the child.

Sing me a bellyful of laughter,
bake me a loaf of sourdough bread,
sew me an oceanful of mermaids,
embroider my shroud when I'm dead.

OVERTURE

Take my hand, you said, on Midsummer's Eve
we'll walk through Finnish pines to an open
space where we'll slip off the everyday
turn off our smartphones, slip on
untried bodies, names, clothes
anything goes

Take my hand, we'll dance on a wooden platform
jump over ditches almost hidden in grass
link arms and circle the biggest fire
you've ever seen, built to burn
the white night through
erase the moon

Take my hand, come on, forget your deadlines
in a land where twilight swallows the stars
and the midnight sun slides down toward
the lake but never sets, there's time
to try out the tango
heaven knows

MY GRANDMOTHER DID NOT SPEAK OF MOTHS

Alone in bed with Hardy
far from the madding crowd
I sense you lousing up the symmetry
of loops and vines on rose-and-tulip walls.

O plain brown moth, solitude-killer,
maker of holes in rugs and clothes,
how dare you flap your raggedness
inside my paraffin lamp?

Domestic pterodactyl, how to stop you?
I douse the flame, close my book
at Hardy's *profound ceiling of stars*
and drift into a heaven under eyelids.

What makes you throw your suicidal body
at the window? Clickety-thug and thug again.
Some prehistoric memory of flame
must be knocking about in your insect brain.

My grandmother who rests in lucky peace
captured dozens of you with her bare fingers,
insensitive to creeping legs on skin,
wings twitching in her cupped palm.

She dropped you in the woodstove. Hundreds of you.
Without skipping a word in her story.
I re-light the lamp, roll a Sunday supplement
into a weapon of moth destruction.

You stumble to the tabletop.
I trap you under cosmopolitan prose.
Smirk to find you bloodless. Nothing wet
on the cloth, merely a brush-away smudge.

I can hear grandma say, *Voi voi voi
kultaseni,* my darling, what a fuss,
it was only one little moth, no mess
nipin napin pieni koi.

Finnish words: *Voi voi voi*—tsk tsk tsk; *kultaseni*—my dear, my darling (from *kulta*: gold); *nipin napin*—barely, only just (idiom, from possessive of 'pinch' + 'button'); *pieni koi*—little moth

DRINKING AT THE STRAY DOG CABARET

St Petersburg, circa 1915

Paint is all very well
but it's messy, you can see
the brush strokes, their shadows
compromise the edges. What I need
is pure colour, straight from the curved
stripes of the rainbow, one hue at a time.

Birds are all very well
but they flap, shit, squawk, coo
their feathers are all different sizes
on their tails, wings, bellies, heads. What I need
is pure flight, suspension in air without noise or wind
an angel without God or gravity, spirit without propellers.

Poetry's all very well
but it rhymes and scans, its lines
strap you into carved Imperial chairs, tie you
to the headboard of a four-poster bed. What I need
is words that never sleep, a futuristic babble, glossolalia
ancient words that only unborn babies understand, pure sound.

Lapdogs are all very well
but they're too docile, eager to listen
to their mistresses, too prim to piss on satin
dresses. I wear leather trousers. What I need
is an untamed bear, roaring as he bursts through the mouth
of his winter cave, clatters through forest and slush, pure hunger.

Rhymes are too docile for untamed birds
to understand babies strapped by leather rainbows
into carved glossolalia. Imperial trousers compromise
the pure hunger of propellers clattering through messy
angel babble. What I need is a four-poster God without noise
a headboard of unborn words that coo and piss but never sleep.

IDAHO WOMEN

'Sing something ugly, Patty, till I get back.'
Dottie strides out of the Sun Valley bar
her rump in narrow Wranglers.

Tiny behind the grand piano
Patty plays Mr. Bojangles
but it doesn't turn out ugly,
her voice husky in the mike.

Patty's all done up tonight—
jet earrings, sequinned dress,
bare shoulders. Her bones
are fine, like a sleek doe's.

Heads of pronghorns,
elk, deer hang on the walls,
trophies of men who hunt—
she sings to their glassy eyes.

Klaus the real estate man,
his belly stuffed in a rugby shirt,
sends Patty a cognac. She leaves it
beside the snifter of ones and fives.

She could be in Vegas but she'll never leave
the mountains—with money from these gigs
she built herself a house up Warm Springs Road,
all wood inside with high ceilings.

On her break she eases past
Klaus's gold-nugget hands,
orders a beer with Dottie. They hug
and chuckle like sharp-tailed grouse,
talk about Patty's new linens from J.C. Penney's,
her bedroom a splash of yellow eyelet cotton.

PEN AND INK

I have never seen your eyes so fierce
but they do not frighten me.
I remember your hint of a wink
when a comic squall on a Routemaster bus
cracked off our strangers' masks.
Now I watch your eyes
intent on my naked body. You could be a surgeon
painting my abdomen with ochre antiseptic,
riveting your gaze on the exact spot
for the scalpel to start the line of blood.
You do not look away
or flinch from drawing every ragged line.
I ache with the strain of rigidity,
long for the women's baths in Helsinki
where we all swam nak'd
(they say it there like waked & slaked)
our breasts and bellies gliding unbound.

On our break we stretch and pace;
you make tea, serve mine
in a cup that says *Make Tea Not War*.
You were a Greenham Common woman
but this is no time for talking.
We listen to Casals play Bach,
I lie prone on your pine floor,
feel the low notes through the wood
from the cello's open throat.
You caught babies in Brazil, cut their cords.
Now you apply pen to paper
with the same clear purpose,
every scar a reason for a line.
When you show me your sketches
it is not to seek approval
but simply to say, these are the results.

MIRACLE ON ESSEX ROAD

She trundled her baby in his pushchair
down the stairs and over the threshold
next to the aquarium and tropical fish shop.

I wondered if her flat was above it or above
the Thai massage parlour on the other side
but asking would have been rude. She locked

her door while I made eyes at her wary baby.
He usually smiles, she said, *but he needs a sleep.
The motion of the pushchair will send him off.*

We walked along, telling the kinds of stories mothers do,
how I had to put away the pram after first snow
and take my daughter in the car. Motion is the cure

for infant insomnia, we agreed. How old is your boy?
*Six months and I'm lucky to have him. We both
nearly died at his birth when my heart gave out.*

My own heart stopped at the story she gave,
unbidden, that mirrored mine over fifty years ago.
We need not speak of miracles, for we embody them.

My firstborn is grown, I told her, and lives in Canada.
We exchanged first names, Julie and I,
two ordinary blessed women on Essex Road.

I can't remember if she said her son's name.
I didn't say my daughter's, but I will now:
Leah Marie, who still loves the motion of cars.

OTHER MOTHERS

Women beyond children,
we make meals for one another,
the pavement between our flats
worn smooth. Halfway home

I pause at the canal. Anonymous
neighbours sleep in narrowboats
locked behind the towpath gate.
I sigh for the dumpling comforts

of your table, your worn sofa's
brandy sadness. A brick bridge

built to deliver the next street
over the canal offers me now
an arch of moonlight
unspooling down the water.

Women beyond husbands,
we mother each other
as grown children
or lovers never can.

At the gate to my basement flat
a panic bird lands on a spike—

the tip of my staircase suddenly
Steeple Point two hundred feet
above the sea, the ridge so narrow
I must place my double feet

in single file. Cliffs drop
vertical from ankle-bones
to surf smashing against rocks.
Where the ridge ends,

the path stops. Heart
flapping in my ears,
I freeze, breath trapped.
I have no one

to come and talk me down
as another mother did, her voice
a safety rope guiding me
each baby step to Duckpool Cove.

EXPECTING NO WELCOME

The harbour was so narrow
it needed three lighthouses
to bring in an ocean liner.

I came across the Atlantic
alone, expecting no welcome,
but emptiness puzzled me.

Tracks on the curved jetty but no train.
Fishing rods cross-hatching
pier-sides but no anglers.
No one spying through binoculars
from windows in the third lighthouse.
Not even milk teeth in the harbour mouth.

I made my own way to the City.

When I needed an inland retreat
my feet inclined to sheep fields,
worn stiles over drystone walls.

No one needs another talisman,
yet a hiking trail gave me
one grey vertebra from a lamb.

Smaller than my palm,
this gargoyle with skinny horns,
horizontal bone corks for ears
and the nose of a pug
invited me to stick my pinkie
through its mouth-hole like a tongue,

conjuring a man in hot and dusty gear.
Shepherd, hiker, hermit, I'll never know:
he tipped his straw hat, walked on by.

INTO THE WEST WITH RAVILIOUS AND YOU

1. Horse from train

By some 'frail travelling coincidence'
we're both assigned the same carriage, third-class,
on a train that takes its time through all the shires
west of London. A Hardy heroine
might keep her eyes fixed on the buttons
sewn to every cross in the upholstery.
A Larkin chick would eye the corduroy nap
on the gentleman's knees an inch away from hers.

I thank the Wessex tribe who scored the biggest
horse I've ever seen into a chalk hill
sidling past this window: here's my chance
to ask you, fellow passenger (your beard
so trim, your eyes a clear, discerning grey)
how a white horse can leap from myth to history.

2. Train from hill

We climbed as far as six mounds of earth
and scree pulled inside out. Foxholes,
we thought. Counted them to catch our breath.

Climbed? You called it ambling, the gradient
friendly. I was more inclined to call it devious,
a steep track up the rampart, long disused.

A signpost loomed, its words weathered
to a ghost warning to hikers and gawkers—
sharp curve ahead. Sheer drop.

Waiting for me to catch up, you counted
carriages on a train whose steam
merged with low clouds, horizon mist.

Years later we discovered Ravilious
had climbed higher, set his easel above
where we stopped. His painting shows

a white horse centre canvas,
eight rabbit holes in the foreground.
How did we miss that giant horse

carved smack in the belly of the hill?

WINTER ANNIVERSARY IN BRUGES

Meet me at the mediaeval bridge
where a red bull flies and grins, a violin
floats above canals and cobbled mazes
where dancers clap and horses draw carriages
full of wedding guests and flowers. The woman
clutching rainbows of wilderness will be me,
arms overflowing with every season in one
bouquet, a blossom for every year since a boy
soprano pleaded the Lord's forgiveness for all
our foolish ways. Snow fell in London, the curate
heard our vows. Your suit was the same dark blue
as my uncle's fiddle, my grandma's spinning wheel.
How can four gut strings and a horsehair bow
play endless variations on snow and rain?

ANONYMOUS 'FLEMISH PRIMITIVE' (ALMOST CERTAINLY MALE) DEPICTS PENTECOST

I give you a woman reading aloud
just as I encountered her,
a halo of stars brooding above
her habit of deepest ultramarine.

In a room of strangers, only she
spoke to me in my village dialect
pronouncing the words of a holy book
written in Latin or possibly German or Greek.

I myself have not been taught to read
but I know this is a time for those who dare
to change old languages into new but why
some are burned alive I do not know.

I give you next eleven men,
whose robes dyed in rainbow lands
where I have never travelled,
gave weeks of joy to my brushes.

Suspended in a hum above the woman
a white dove dropped beads of flame
from its beak, dispersed them in the room
with its wingtips, like seeds over fields.

A single fire-bubble came to rest above
each man's head—the cradle of thought
as my mother said—and each man held his tongue
while the woman in blue read aloud.

Eleven pairs of men's hands, weaponless
traced the air with improvised
finger-songs, gestures of openness.
I am not deaf but I heard the silence of peace.

Those who entered next were my patrons,
a Bruges banker and his wife, severe
in black garments of understatement:
layers of silk, wool, velvet, sable.

I could not tell whether strangers
in their entrance hall surprised them:
I have noticed the powerful and wealthy
are inclined to keep their poise.

I do not know if their ears heard the words
of the woman in blue, or their eyes saw the bird
but the air above their heads remained empty
as they knelt. I give you a true likeness of their faces.

YOU ASKED GOD FOR A DREAM

but He gave it to me: a baby spoke
in sentences, articulate and serious.

Only 15 months old but already a charmer
unaware of her beauty or power,
she opened her rosebud lips,
revealed the tips of her baby teeth
and delivered a disquisition to her mum.

I can't remember the subject—was it
observation, argument or narrative?

But I'll never forget how her baby tongue
rolled its Rs and trilled its Ls ever so slightly.
Entirely calm, she was absorbed in making sounds,
shaping them into words and joined-up sentences.

Wise beyond her weeks and months,
she did not seek attention or approval
from her grandparents or mother,
their doting a gift she acknowledged with a nod.

I was the stranger in the room who neither
frightened nor interested this dream baby.
She simply spoke her marvellous sentences
as if she were the only person listening.

When I awoke and came downstairs
I saw that the baby had your face
and a poise you said you had prayed for:
a sign from God to give you
fluency and strength.
I need them too.

GOATFELL, ISLE OF ARRAN

After an etching by Craigie Aitchison

Pared from a baby's fingernail,
the sickle moon begins the winter equinox.
The last boat in knows its way through darkness.

An invisible wife in the fisherman's cottage
stokes the stove, a smoke thread rising
from her roof, another from his trawler flue,

ropes that reach for a single tree, leafless,
that stretches the Y of its limbs
toward the cone of Goatfell, purple

against a black sky. We try for narrative
and find two white scratches, a possible
cross on the mountain's far side.

HER FAMILY

After Barbara Hepworth

She built a set of ancestors on wire
armatures, moulded them with plaster,
wet her hands, slapped the backs, bellies,
limbs of parents, children, all her kin;
smoked a fag and wished her tribe good night:

Dry slowly, my people, do not crack or weep,
stay strong and harden in your sleep.

When they were ripe she set to carving torsos,
muscles and faces, rasping skin. Brushing off
flakes and dust, she carted her people to the foundry,
filled their hollows with liquid bronze.

Her family stands at Snape, far from the edge
of the marsh, where earth gives way to reeds.
They need no plinth; they occupy the land.

Nor do they mourn her accidental death.
Cold bronze eyes are not designed for grief.

III

My working eye is muscled
With a curious tension ...
Trusting in its vision
Even should it see
The holy holy spirit gambol
Counterheadwise,
Lithe and warm as any animal.
— Anne Wilkinson

SHADOW IN HADLEIGH

January sags and we go hunting
snowdrops. Years of habit.

Today on a sodden riverside path
a black lab cross wandered up to us
slow as an old dog. Not a jumper.
Left our coats free of mud or slobber.
Shadow's her name, her man said.
Only five years old but born mournful.

But why did she suddenly race around that tree?
Sniff of rat or toad? *Moment of madness*, her man said.

The river had swallowed a month of rain,
then flooded woods and fields last week.
Acres of stale water, muck—no blooms
for us to find this year. *Hang on*, you said.

On a peat island the size of a rubber boot: one clump
of snowdrops. Rare as baby teeth in an old man's grin.

Shadow and her man long gone
plodding up their routine path
we cut loose, my man and I,
twirled and splashed in the mud.
Mad dogs can teach old bones, I guess,
how to kick it up. Make it spring.

AT THE ELBOW OF PISSARRO

The level railway-crossing keeper's wife
        is hanging
every shade of laundered whites, her line
        suspended
from middle-up-the-willow-sapling branches
        on opposite sides
of Chiswick's most luxuriant kitchen garden

A straw-stuffed mannequin in flapping rags
        knee-deep
in turnip, carrot, runner bean and corn tops
        scares off
pigeon, magpie, crow and starling
        scavengers. A baby
crawls toward a chicken coop, a clutter of beaks
        pick-picking
at eggshells, grit, snails, beetles, hencorn

A woven willow fence divides the wife's not quite
        unkempt
enclosure from cricketers, almost static on the common
        she pauses
to gaze at their whites, their bats, the pairs of stumps
        the measured
way they move like bits of minuets
        broken
by episodes of willow-crack on leather

The midday train pulls up, as if tripping a switch
        for gongs
from a clock-tower so far away the spire's a single
        hair-stroke
of paint on a thimble church the same brick-red
        as her shirtwaist

A fielder, transfixed by the stopped carriages
        glimpses in a gap
her cinnabar bodice between the linens
        she's pinning up

The painter and I watch them from the footbridge
        two lives split
by a hand-made fence of twigs and air, flexible as leather
        yet impossible
to breach. The train pulls away, its engine and whistle
        dissolve
fade into the baby's yodel

VISION ON PLATFORM 2

I didn't realize I was reading
Seamus Heaney's poems in *Seeing Things*
on the very day the Irish honour the holy
St Patrick. Let me assure you, he has no role
in this tale. A man with dreadlocks sitting
beside me on Platform 1 at Seven Sisters,
next stop Rectory Road, raised his eyes

from his smartphone and, lo, the moment
I looked up from *Seeing Things,* a vision
on Platform 2 appeared to us both. 'Behold'
we would have said, but strangers never speak
at Seven Sisters. Our mouths fell open
at a row of seven nuns in black habits,
seven immaculate white wimples.

Above their heads the sign read 'Seven Sisters'
in ordinary railway font, sans serif upper case,
a photo-opportunity from heaven, a miracle
for all commuters save the nuns, their eyes
on bibles or fingers on beads. They didn't know
that a Hackney cousin of Robert Doisneau
had captured them forever on his smartphone,

silent, upon a bench at Seven Sisters.
His shot went viral on facebook and twitter,
enchanting all save a pair of literal souls
who believed they spied an extra holy knee
draped in black, or an eighth sister's elbow.
Who would accuse a man who never cuts
his hair of cropping a redundant nun?

I was there that morning and I swear
that only and exactly seven sisters sat
beneath that sign, a sevenfold blessing.
Let no one mock this miracle of symmetry.
Let no one credit photoshop, St Patrick
or the inspiration of Seamus Heaney's
'squarings, crossings, lightenings or settings'.

HER HABIT

Bobbing at the level
of anybody else's waist, her face
pulled her body string-wise,
like a wooden toy on wheels.

Our eyes dropped, our fingers traced
veins on marble tables, rivers of rust,
clouds with irrelevant names—
cirrus, nacreous, nimbostratus.

Cigarette smoke, that fat smog, ate talk:
you could have heard a mouse cough.

A blur of grey slid toward the bar.
Doubled under gabardine, oh her spine.
What can be done with the halt and lame?

The barman knew her, poured four thumbs
of *mirto rosso,* sweet and strong,
that Sardinian shot from the dark red berries
of myrtle bushes that crowd out the briers

in Isaiah. Like a swallower of knives
or fireballs, she threw back her head,
downed the liqueur, her crucifix bouncing.

Slow as a turtle's head from a shell-hole,
her hand proceeded out of its sleeve
to situate her empty shot-glass on the bar,
high as an altar, with practised grace.

Suddenly her spine, it came unhinged
and her body, well, it melted
down to the terracotta floor,
handy spot to park her hold-all.

We can see she's done this before:
unzip a flap, extract a battered envelope,
count out coins in small denominations—

the clock shows 4:54—
straighten wimple, glide over cobbled piazza
to Santa Maria Maggiore, without a cane.

Lord, when I'm old, let me be so quick,
so neat in my daily needs.
Let me take my ritual nip
without a fuss, wordless.

IN SEARCH OF UPLIFT

Margaret Street, London W1

It was heaven to sit in that shop
at number 28, reading tomes
at a vast table, its buttersoft leather top
stained with ink and sweat;

to stack up model prayers,
radical theologies, translations
of scriptures to compare.
Sticklers dug lines into my forehead.

Squinting at footnotes, I twisted
the brass neck of a lamp adapted
for electricity when Agatha Christie
had never been kissed, when girls

floated to ladyhood, their eyes
lowered, barely nodding at puberty.
What is epiphany but surprise
when mystery is revealed.

Last night at All Saints next door, the queen
of crime novelists, PD James in thick tweed,
recited an unsolved mystery: word made flesh.
She was a mouthpiece, nothing more.

Spiritual dust and bliss: that was Mowbrays.
Now the shop sells brassieres. Women squeeze
into cubicles with giggling kindred spirits,
an uplift earthier by far than cardinals

or desert fathers ever could have known.
One velvet-cushioned hour in the queue
and my spirits will rise when a fitter proves
that clever lace can make this old flesh new.

HOW TO TRANSLATE JOY

Here we are at the knee page, the jeweller's page,
indeed, a page of joy, so let us juggle words
for joy is the root of all jewellery.

Do not sneer: all the toys are skittish here
for this is a page of greed and gambling,
indeed, since yesterday everything's at stake.

We can while away the hours leafing through
this Japanese garden, count irises and hyacinths
or sleep like dormice until the fiddlers come.

Here the javelin-throwers are greedy for thrills,
jolly for gin, comical as journalists
in Jordan who never can speak-it the lingoese.

Already they are sinking under yellow paper,
jiggling their knees like jelly babies,
throwing away their careers-o.

Here the newsagent grows junipers in jars,
shuffles melds and games of gin rummy,
gambles for knick-knacks in jade.

Here the gymnast goes to grammar school,
the jaguar springs from cage to kindergarten,
the fiddler bangs his knee on a broomstick.

A poem made from words found on page 135 of
The Collins Paperback Italian Dictionary, 1989

EVERY SEVENTH STARLING

Ever since Pliny the Elder we have asked
why a flock of starlings will suddenly
change course and consciousness,
spatter and consecrate the twilight
with the wonder of murmurations.

Why a cloud of starlings chooses to spiral
over fields or seas before they roost, as if
a gust of melody keeps them up and away
from the safety of pier struts or leafless trees.

Why they sweep the air as one collective mind,
thousands of birds following every seventh starling
as it winks and tips, like a magnet pulling
iron filings into new lines and shapes.

Millennia later, scientists can measure
the how but not the why of such behaviour.
We might imagine it as metanoia of the heart,
the way these birds inscribe our several
longings, our turnings. Apart, together, apart.

GOLDFINCH

The first cup I chose was labelled love,
a goldfinch painted on a willow tip,
but what I overlooked was the spot
of blood on its beak. The china cracked
and bitterness poured out, burning
my hand, staining my silk kimono.
The second cup I chose was porcelain,
'No regrets' painted above a Piaf who sang
as I swallowed gin, laughed and wept.
Now my chosen cup is blown glass,
empty, glacier-blue, full of peace.

FIFTEENTH SWAN

A sonnet of swans, each with its own line and wake,
swam toward us at low tide as we walked
the disused rails, the crackbone cobblestones
from Lockyers Quay round Sutton Harbour and back.

A quartet of lads, variously bearded, lounged
on a Jaguar bonnet, rucksacks leaning against
its chrome wheels. Laughed, smoked, swanned about,
oblivious to the red-faced man on his mobile phone.

A man on a bike told us his roles for the Fishermen's Mission:
Chat with the jobless, the homeless, drunks sleeping it off.
Visit survivors of storms like ex-hurricane Ophelia:

waning, she still had the strength to sink a trawler,
drown the captain's father. His widow told me she gazed
into a whirlpool that night, saw the fifteenth swan

carry her man into the black river of death.

HONEYMOON FLIGHT, CIRCA 1934

This is our honeymoon, so far so true.
We packed light: a single valise between us,
my new vanity case. Only the essentials
for a long weekend in Tripoli.

We leave on a wing and a whispered vow
never to return to Rome, our jobs
in plush quarters, hush-hush.
Never again to follow orders

or smile at puffed-up little bosses.
Never again to see our village homes
or feast at our mammas' tables. To praise
Il Duce for his gifts to Italy? Never again.

Yes, we are grateful for his first-class
tickets on Ala Littoria, his new airline,
that magnificent baby, futuristical, snappy,
better than any in Europe, even the world!

We will never forget his greasy speech
at our wedding feast, his liquid praises
to the bride. I'd rather have drowned
with a dozen virgins than listen to more.

When we are safe in the air we will laugh,
free as swifts or swallows, even eagles!
Not yet. We are still on the tarmac,
hat brims down, chins to chests,

your hands jammed deep in the pockets
of your trenchcoat, your belt knotted
tight as the grip I must keep on my
blood-red handbag. Such soft kid.

SUNDAY MORNING IN BERGAMO WITH DAMON

> *Hark how the mower Damon sung,*
> *With love of Juliana stung!*
> *While everything did seem to paint*
> *The scene more fit for his complaint.*
> – Andrew Marvell

My uncle told me of soldiers
picked off as they crept from trenches,
cut down as they ran in the wrong

uniforms clotted with mud.
The old fellow's gone a year, left me
flat and chattels. Some garden.

My stubble itches. I need to mow
the grass on this narrow strip of land.
The sun's already blazing

but I left my Ray-Bans in Milan.
Juliana, my bride, gets to lie in bed
while I'm sweating and swearing,

pulling the fraying cord of this rotary mower.
Here's an overgrown path, worn bricks a foot apart.
I'll clean them off for Juliana's feet. So touchable.

Damn I've stubbed my toe on a buried tufa stone.
Those cedar tops have gone ragged, lack point.
Need some clippers. Where's a ladder.

That maddening church. The electronic carillon
keeps pummeling some hymn into my head
in endless loops. Something I knew as a child.

Make me a channel of your peace,
where there is hatred let me bring your love.
I always liked those words of Brother Francis.

Allora, vediamo. Hack the ivy from this grotto
my uncle built, kneel down to rescue
the red lamp, a guttered candle in its bowl.

Get rid of the grey plastic roses plugging the mouth
of this cracked maiolica vase. I can just make out
letters on its base—*A Juliana.*

O Mio Dio. Here's a tissue to dab away
cobwebs and dirt caked on the virgin's face,
stand her upright in the grotto,

its roots deeper than any alp,
far too heavy for me to haul away.
Juliana may mock. Let it stay.

A SOLDIER PONDERS THE LIMITS OF ARITHMETIC

Numbers can measure song but cannot sing.
Their little metal vocal cords can only
squeeze into the space between a bullet
and its barrel, or the trigger and its finger.

Numbers have no heart for playing, soft
or hard, their clock-hearts always fail to find
a rhythm beyond tap-drip from a lime-encrusted
faucet, or the patter of hail on a quonset hut.

Numbers never dance unless their boots
can shake off marching orders, kick off the mud-clods
that stick to their soles, break a soldier's pace,
make his heart-rate accelerate across no-man's land.

STONES ON TRIAL

For Eddie Ladd, 'Gaza/Blaenannerch'

We watch your lone thin muscular body negotiate stones,
some in a random arrangement as though dropped onstage
with bones of dead species by a flood in retreat,

others aligned like temple ruins or towns
that desert winds have uncovered, then abandoned
in sand and grit under your naked feet.

Unmanned drones whine in the test skies of Wales.
You dance into being landscapes that swell, sigh and fall
from your Ceredigion home farm to a tent camp in Gaza.

Unnamed targets never know until it's too late.
Your body leans into postures of interrogation:
'Stones, what are your politics?'

'What is your history, religion?'
'Who owns you, numbers you?'
Mouthless, eyeless, the stones refuse to say.

You pile them in wobbly columns, climb them
in sequence, balance one stubborn leg on each.
Their submission is temporary. You smash

these make-do pedestals, place a single stone
on your bare spine, bend straight from the hips,
your body forced to crawl. Again, again, again.

The bigger stones you heft, drag, push, pile
at the base of a polished wall too high to scale.
You run up the stones, hurl yourself at the wall.

Grim and pitiless, its steel sides dig into your hands
as your female body ascends inch by inch, a desperate
twitching crucifix of bone and tethered skin.

THE CAPE AND THE STEEPLE

He strides along in tennis shoes and cape
to visit us in Cross Street, Islington.
His cape is plain black cloth—
no purple, blue or scarlet stuff
woven with gold like Aaron's priestly robe,
no rows of precious stones
exotic as sardius,
astonishing as carbuncle,
common as diamonds.

He strides along in tennis shoes and cape
around St Mary's parish, a gathering of streets
so small his cape could almost cover it, as if he'd pitched a tent
across our neighbourhood, strong pegs to hold down
flapping sounds of lorries, cars,
a fire engine, ambulance, police.

A tent with gaps to let in everyone:
God has no edges or limits.

This cape has been a blanket for the homeless,
a comforter for those who cannot sleep,
a tablecloth for formal meals and picnics,
a flourish for artists, actors, other oddballs,
a dignity for those who mete out laws,
a loving clarity for those who break them,
a space for those pushed into corners,
a hide and seeking place for kids.

As he takes down his cape from its hook
in the heart of our parish to walk elsewhere,
what can we people give him?
There's the steeple—a needle
to thread the sky and sew him a cape
of stuff so rare and blue,
uncommon as an ordinary prayer.

FEAST

Three wise women arrived bearing gifts

Gardeners, they offered from the earth

What their hands had tended, tied, harvested
                               (not without pain)
Apples and pears from an Okanagan orchard
                               (crouch lift stretch ache)
Honey from hives on the edge of the Grizzly Trail
                               (buzz claw lacerate sting)
Walnuts from a grandfather tree in the Dordogne
                               (hammer gnarl yelp crack)
Pilgrims, settlers, cooks, the earth's midwives
                               (blood steam linen wool straw)
They brought strudel, baklava, tarte tatin
                               (gingerbread black as tar)
For the Christmas feast: spice and bite
                               (grace fat gold leaf)
For sweetness on tooth and tongue
                               (breathe in breathe out)
For the soothness of Amen

NOTES

Wading for stones (p. 3)
Wesakechak is a First Nations name for the god of creation, god of waterways, trickster god.

Reveen the Impossibilist (p. 14)
Peter J. Reveen (1935-2013) was a stage illusionist and hypnotist who emigrated from Australia to Canada in 1961. As Reveen the Impossibilist he toured for 35 years, mainly in Canada, eventually performing to over 6 million people across North America.

Expecting no welcome (p. 38)
The first three stanzas are after "Newhaven Harbour" [1937] by Eric Ravilious.

Into the west with Ravilious and you (p. 39)
After "Train Landscape" [1939] and "The Westbury Horse" [1939] by Eric Ravilious.

Anonymous 'Flemish Primitive' (almost certainly male) depicts Pentecost (p. 42)
After "Pentecost" [c. 1489] by the Flemish painter known only as the 'Master of the Baroncelli portraits'. In the Groeninge Museum, Bruges.

At the elbow of Pissarro (p. 50)
After "View Across Stamford Brook Common" [1897] by Camille Pissarro.

Epigraphs
by Anna Akhmatova, from "In 1940", tr. Richard McKane 1989
by Gwendolyn MacEwen, from "Dark Pines under Water" 1969
by Andrew Marvell, from "Damon the Mower" 1681
by P.K. Page, from "The Stenographers" 1946
by Anne Wilkinson, from "Lens" 1955

AUTHOR BIOGRAPHY

Nancy Mattson moved from the Canadian prairies to London in 1990. Her previous three collections are *Finns and Amazons* (Arrowhead 2012), which begins with poems about early 20th century Russian women artists but moves to a search for her Finnish great-aunt who disappeared in Stalinist Russia; *Writing with Mercury* (Flambard 2006); and *Maria Breaks Her Silence* (Coteau 1989), shortlisted for Canada's Gerald Lampert Award. She co-organises Poetry in the Crypt in Islington, north London.